CW01213121

Original title:
In the Glow of Winter's Flame

Copyright © 2024 Creative Arts Management OÜ
All rights reserved.

Author: Evelyn Hartman
ISBN HARDBACK: 978-9916-94-414-1
ISBN PAPERBACK: 978-9916-94-415-8

Candlelight Conversations

In the glow of flickering light,
Whispers weave through the night.
Secrets shared in tender tones,
Hearts explore their quiet zones.

Gentle laughter fills the air,
Promises made without a care.
Every moment feels so right,
Captured in the soft twilight.

The Solstice Serenade

Underneath the winter moon,
Nature sings a timeless tune.
Stars align in cosmic dance,
As the world takes a chance.

Snowflakes twirl in soft embrace,
Whispered wonders fill the space.
Joyful hearts beat in the chill,
Time stops, and dreams are still.

Flames of Hope and Kindness

A spark ignites in the dark,
Lighting paths with a warm mark.
Hands reach out, a gentle guide,
In the flames, we do abide.

Together we rise, hearts aglow,
Sharing love as it flows.
Kindness blooms in every heart,
From the flames, we will not part.

Ashen Echoes of Longing

In the quiet of the night,
Memories fade from sight.
Echoes whisper soft and low,
Yearning for what we don't know.

Through the haze of soft regret,
Dreams linger, never met.
In the shadows, hope's a spark,
Guiding us through the dark.

Reflections in the Candlestick

In shadows dance, the light does play,
Mirrored thoughts, lost in the sway.
A gentle flicker, warm and bright,
Echoes of dreams in the soft night.

Time stands still, secrets unfold,
Wisps of whispers, stories told.
In golden glow, our hearts align,
Candlestick visions, yours and mine.

Snowbound Radiance

Blankets of white, serene and wide,
Whispers of winter, none can hide.
Stars above in a frosty embrace,
Nature's quiet, a softened space.

Footprints trail through the silent night,
Each step a story, pure delight.
In snowbound realms, we find our peace,
Radiant stillness, a sweet release.

The Quiet Flame's Embrace

A flickering glow, serene and warm,
In the stillness, it begins to charm.
Each ember tells of moments past,
In the quiet, memories cast.

Wrapped in warmth, we pause and sigh,
The flame's embrace, our spirits fly.
In hushed whispers, secrets blend,
A timeless dance that will not end.

Kindred Spirits in the Firelight

Around the fire, our laughter soars,
Flickering shadows dance on the floors.
With every crackle, hearts ignite,
Kindred spirits in the warm light.

Stories shared in the glowing gleam,
In this moment, we dare to dream.
Bound by the warmth, we share the night,
In the firelight, all is right.

Embers of Frost's Embrace

In the night, shadows dance slow,
Cold winds whisper secrets below.
Frosted stars twinkle bright,
Embers flicker, chasing the night.

Moonlit paths, a silvery sheen,
Nature's canvas, a tranquil scene.
Beneath the chill, warmth still glows,
Embers of life where beauty flows.

Alone we wander, yet we find,
In frost's arms, so gently kind.
Love's warmth against the bitter air,
Embers whisper, always there.

Through frozen branches, dreams aspire,
Hearts ignite with hidden fire.
In each breath, a story told,
Embers of frost, a heart so bold.

Illuminated Whispers of the Cold

Whispers carried on icy beams,
Silent echoes of fragile dreams.
Stars emerge in a crisp night,
Illuminating shadows in flight.

A breath reveals a fleeting mist,
In the dark, memories persist.
Cold's embrace, a beckoning call,
Softly spoken, we stand enthralled.

In frost-laden fields, silence grows,
Underneath, a warmth still glows.
A tapestry woven by chill and light,
Illuminated whispers take flight.

In the depth of winter's heart,
A spark of longing, a tender start.
Through every flake that softly falls,
Whispers of warmth break winter's walls.

A Hearth's Warmth Beneath Snow

Beneath the blanket of purest white,
A hearth flickers, banishing night.
Crackling wood, a symphony's cheer,
The warmth of home is drawing near.

Snowflakes dance in the gentle breeze,
Outside, the world is brought to its knees.
Inside the glow, we gather near,
A hearth's warmth dissolves all fear.

Tales are spun of olden days,
Laughter echoes, as joy stays.
With every sip, the cold fades away,
Under the roof, we cherish the day.

Memories' warmth against the frost,
In the hearth's comfort, we find what's lost.
Together we stand, against the cold,
A hearth's warmth, a story bold.

Flickering Dreams of Ice and Fire

In the twilight, sparks fly high,
A world painted 'neath the icy sky.
Flickering dreams, both bold and bright,
Dance with shadows, embracing the night.

Through frozen breath and glistening grass,
We chase the warmth, let the moments pass.
Fire's glow warms the chill of fate,
As we gather, it's never too late.

Each dream a flame, fierce and alive,
In the heart's glow, we truly strive.
To blend the ice with embers near,
Flickering whispers of hope appear.

As night deepens, let passions soar,
Together we'll find what we're longing for.
In dreams of ice and fire we find,
A place where our souls are intertwined.

Frosty Nights and Candlelit Dreams

The night is crisp, a breath of air,
Stars like diamonds, shining rare.
Candle flames dance, flicker bright,
Whispers of warmth in frosty light.

Shadows stretch across the floor,
Memories linger, tales of yore.
Wrapped in blankets, hearts aglow,
Frosty nights, where dreams shall flow.

A Tapestry of Warm and Cold

Threads of warmth weave through the chill,
A quilt of comfort, soft and still.
Winter's breath, a gentle bite,
Contrasts bloom in day and night.

Candles flicker, shadows play,
In the tapestry, night meets day.
Woven tales of hearts entwined,
In this fabric, love defined.

Glowing Paths Through White Silence

Footsteps crunch on snow so deep,
Whispers echo, the world's asleep.
Guided by lanterns, softly glowed,
Through the white, a path is strode.

Silence reigns, a soothing balm,
In winter's grasp, the air feels calm.
Nature's canvas, pure and bright,
Glowing paths, a wondrous sight.

Ember Hues in the Wintry Gaze

Embers flicker, softly warm,
In winter's clutch, a gentle charm.
Through frosted panes, the world appears,
A vibrant dance that stirs the years.

Laughter echoes, joy ignites,
In the heart of these cold nights.
Embers twinkle like the stars,
In wintry gazes, love is ours.

Glowing Reflections in Winter's Mirror

In twilight's grasp, the world grows still,
A mirror formed of ice and chill.
The stars above begin to gleam,
While shadows dance, a silent dream.

Each flake that falls, a whispered tale,
Of journeys past, of hearts that sail.
Among the trees, the whispers flow,
As winter's breath begins to glow.

Cascade of Light Through the Winter Pines

Beneath the boughs of ancient trees,
A cascade flows, a gentle breeze.
With light that dances, pure and bright,
In winter's heart, a wondrous sight.

The needles shimmer, catching fire,
A symphony of hope, desire.
Through branches bare, the sunbeams play,
Transforming night into the day.

Kindling Courage in the Icy Twilight

In twilight's grip, the coldness grows,
But courage blooms where silence flows.
Each heartbeat echoes, strong and true,
Lighting the paths that we pursue.

Amidst the frost, our spirits rise,
With every challenge, the heart defies.
In icy breath, we find our song,
A call to stand, to be more strong.

The Glittering Ember of Introspection

In quiet moments, shadows fade,
An ember glows, where thoughts are laid.
Reflecting deep, we seek to find,
The whispered truths of heart and mind.

With every flicker, wisdom grows,
And in the night, the stillness flows.
Through introspection, lights ignite,
Guiding our way through darkest night.

The Last Glow Before the Frost

Golden leaves drift down,
Whispers of the autumn's song.
Beneath the setting sun,
A fleeting warmth, not lasting long.

The horizon blushes bright,
As shadows stretch and fall.
Nature holds its breath in peace,
Awaiting winter's call.

The chill begins to creep,
Through branches bare and stark.
Yet in this soft goodbye,
Lingers still a glowing spark.

Time dances on the edge,
Of seasons swiftly passing by.
The last glow fades away,
Like a lover's tender sigh.

Warm Threads Woven in a Winter's Night

In the hearth, the flames do glow,
Casting shadows on the wall.
We wrap in blankets soft and warm,
Listening to the winter's call.

Outside, the snowflakes flutter down,
Like whispers of a silent dream.
Inside, we weave our tales of love,
In the gentle glow that seems.

Each thread a memory spun,
Binding hearts in cozy light.
With every stitch, we find our peace,
In the warmth of the winter's night.

As the world sleeps hushed and still,
Our laughter echoes hand in hand.
In this moment we create,
A tapestry so grand.

Flames that Dance with Snowflakes

In the night, the fires burn,
Embers twinkling, fierce and bright.
Outside, the snowflakes swirl and play,
A ballet of the dark and light.

The warmth surrounds us, a soft embrace,
As frost kisses the window's pane.
We watch the world transform in white,
In this winter's wonderland, unchained.

Each flame leaps up to meet the stars,
Echoing calls from the cold unknown.
With every spark, a wish takes flight,
In the glow, we're never alone.

Together we bask in this radiant warmth,
As snowflakes fall, a gentle show.
In the fire's light, our spirits dance,
Flames that meld with snowflakes' flow.

The Quiet Fire of the Longest Night

The longest night wraps round the earth,
A blanket of stillness, a soft sigh.
In the dark, a quiet fire glows,
Warming hearts as the hours pass by.

Beneath the stars, we find our peace,
In stories shared, and dreams unspun.
The fire crackles, a gentle sound,
In the silence, we are one.

Outside, the winter's breath is cold,
But inside, love's flame ignites.
Together we embrace the dark,
Guided by the fire's light.

As night whispers tenderly,
And the world slows its pace of flight,
We hold on to this tranquil moment,
The quiet fire of the longest night.

Serenity Beneath the Shimmer

Under the moon's soft glow,
Waves whisper secrets low.
Stars twinkle in the night,
Painting dreams in silver light.

Gentle breezes softly play,
Carrying worries away.
Silent reflections float near,
In this calm, all is clear.

Ripples dance on the lake,
Echoes of the heart awake.
Floating thoughts drift like leaves,
Caught in joy, the spirit believes.

In this space so divine,
Peace wraps around like a vine.
Serenity calls me close,
Beneath the shimmer, I repose.

Whispers Through the Cranberry Woods

Cranberry vines stretch so wide,
Secrets of the forest reside.
Leaves rustle with soft delight,
Guiding shadows through the night.

Birdsong flutters on the breeze,
Nature hums with graceful ease.
Sunlight filters through the trees,
Whispers dance upon the leaves.

Footsteps here lead me where,
Mysteries linger in the air.
Each turn reveals a new sight,
Nature's heart beats warm and bright.

Lost in hues of scarlet dreams,
The forest sings with silent themes.
In this earthy, sacred space,
I find solace, warm embrace.

The Spark of Belonging

In the warmth of shared laughter,
Hearts unite, joy thereafter.
Connections sparkling like fire,
Fueling hopes and sweet desires.

With each story told anew,
Threads of friendship weave on through.
Trust and love begin to grow,
In this bond, our spirits glow.

Hands held tight in times of need,
In this garden, we plant seed.
Together facing every storm,
Creating refuge, safe and warm.

The spark ignites, brightly shines,
In the dance of heart and minds.
A tapestry of dreams unfolds,
In the warmth, our life molds.

Illuminating the Wintry Path

Snowflakes fall like whispered dreams,
Transforming earth in silver gleams.
Footprints mark the journey made,
As the wintry skies cascade.

Frosty breath paints the air,
Magic lingers everywhere.
Twilight casts a gentle glow,
Lighting paths through depths of snow.

Each step sings a quiet tune,
Beneath the watchful, crescent moon.
Nature's breath, serene and pure,
Guides the heart to feel secure.

In this stillness, warmth ignites,
Hope emerges in fading lights.
The wintry path, though cold and stark,
Leads us home, igniting spark.

A Midnight Glow in a Winter's Tale

The snowflakes dance in flight,
Whispers of a frosty night.
Moonlight spills on frozen ground,
In the stillness, magic found.

Icicles hang like crystal dreams,
Reflecting soft silver beams.
The world is hushed, wrapped in white,
A serenade of pure delight.

Footprints trace the silent way,
Leading to where shadows play.
Stars shimmer in velvet skies,
While the heartache gently dies.

In this winter's tender glow,
Hope ignites, and spirits grow.
A midnight calm, a heartfelt sigh,
A moment framed beneath the sky.

Nature's Lullaby in Candlelight

The flames dance low, a gentle sway,
Creating warmth at the end of day.
Outside, the world is dark and deep,
But here within, the shadows sleep.

Flickering light on crimson walls,
Echoes of the forest calls.
Inhale the scent of pine and earth,
Nature sings of quiet birth.

A lullaby of whispering leaves,
With every note, the spirit breathes.
Crickets chirp in sweet refrain,
As candlelight beats back the pain.

The night unfolds with every flame,
Each flicker soft, yet never tame.
In this cocoon of golden hue,
The heart finds peace, a love anew.

Under the Canopy of Stars

A blanket tossed across the night,
Each star a spark, a tiny light.
Under this vast celestial dome,
A quiet soul may find a home.

Whispers of the cosmos swirl,
In stillness, dreams begin to twirl.
Galaxies hidden, worlds unknown,
Silent stories, ever shone.

The moon, a watchful guardian bright,
Bathes the earth in silver light.
Crickets serenade the air,
As magic blooms, rare and fair.

Beneath this stretch, hearts intertwine,
Lost in wonder, yet so divine.
Each fleeting moment flows like art,
In this embrace, a beating heart.

A Choreography of Light and Chill

Frosty breath in the frigid air,
Nature's dance, a subtle affair.
Glistening glades where shadows steep,
Light and chill in harmony leap.

The sun breaks through with golden grace,
Its warmth igniting the coldest space.
Branches sway in a soft ballet,
As winter bids the night to stay.

Twinkling lights on frosted trees,
Whisper tales on the winter breeze.
Each moment captured, pure and free,
In this choreography of glee.

Nature spins a tale so bright,
Of darkened skies and soft daylight.
In every breath, in every thrill,
A timeless dance of light and chill.

The Ember's Embrace

In the glow of fading light,
The embers dance, warm and bright.
Whispers of the night unfold,
Stories shared, both new and old.

Crackling wood sings a song,
In this haven, we belong.
Hearts alight with love's embrace,
Time stands still in this safe space.

Frost-Kissed Radiance

Morning breaks with frosty breath,
Nature wrapped in winter's wreath.
Each flake glimmers, pure and white,
A world transformed, a wondrous sight.

Pine trees dusted, standing tall,
Whispers of the snowflakes' call.
Footsteps crunch on crystal ground,
In this magic, joy is found.

Warmth Amidst the Chill

Outside the world wears icy seams,
Inside, we share our hopes and dreams.
With every laugh, the cold retreats,
As love surrounds, the heart still beats.

Brimming mugs and cozy throws,
The fire's flicker gently glows.
In this shelter from the storm,
We find a way to feel the warm.

Hearthside Dreams

By the fire, our spirits soar,
Tales of old and evermore.
Whispers drift on scented air,
Hearthside dreams, we freely share.

Stars peek through the window's glass,
Time slips by, moments pass.
In the warmth, our worries cease,
Bathed in love, we find our peace.

A Canvas of Crystalline Dreams

In twilight's glow, the stars align,
Soft whispers brush the edge of time.
A canvas blank, in silver light,
Awakens dreams that soar in flight.

With every stroke, a story spun,
The heartbeats race, together, as one.
A symphony of colors bright,
In crystalline worlds, we find our sight.

Through fields of hope, we gently tread,
Each step a path where souls are led.
In this embrace, our wishes gleam,
A canvas stretched with endless dream.

The night unfolds, a magic realm,
Where all is guided by love's helm.
Together we chase the starlit seams,
In this canvas, our crystalline dreams.

Winter's Flickering Choir

In frosty air, a whisper sings,
As nature dons her jeweled rings.
The silence breaks with subtle cheer,
A flickering choir draws us near.

Each flake descends, a soft ballet,
An icy melody on display.
The moonlight bathes the world in grace,
As shadows dance in winter's embrace.

With every note, the cold ignites,
Warm spirits rise on starry nights.
Beneath the boughs, our laughter swirls,
In winter's grip, a song unfurls.

Together we share this gentle bliss,
A harmony that none can miss.
With hands entwined against the chill,
We find our joy in winter's thrill.

Glowing Hearts in the Frosty Night

In the stillness, shadows play,
Beneath a sky of endless gray.
Yet in the dark, a light we find,
With glowing hearts, our hopes aligned.

Each breath released in winter's air,
Transforms the silence into prayer.
A flicker warms the coldest space,
As love ignites a tender grace.

We stroll through dreams, hand in hand,
Finding warmth in the snow-kissed land.
With every step, our spirits rise,
In frosty night, our laughter flies.

Though winter's chill may bite and gnaw,
Together, we find a brighter thaw.
Our glowing hearts will light the way,
In the frost, we'll dance, we'll sway.

Collecting Moments by the Fire

By the crackling fire we gather near,
With stories shared and voices clear.
Collecting moments, rich and bright,
In the warmth that fills the night.

The flames flicker, shadows dance,
Time slows down, a golden chance.
We sip our joys, let silence speak,
In this stillness, the heart feels weak.

Outside, the world is cold and stark,
But here, we build our glowing spark.
With laughter ringing, spirits soar,
Each moment cherished, we crave for more.

As embers fade, and stars ignite,
We'll hold these memories, pure delight.
Collecting moments, a treasure trove,
By the fire's glow, our hearts will rove.

Radiance Amongst the Chill

In twilight's grasp, the snowflakes fall,
Gentle whispers, winter's call.
A glow emerges, soft and bright,
Painting dreams in pale moonlight.

With every breath, a frosty sigh,
As stars awaken in the sky.
A silken warmth beneath the cold,
In dreams of warmth, our hearts unfold.

The lanterns flicker, hope's embrace,
In deep winter, we find our grace.
Though shadows stretch, horizon's glow,
Radiant love warms the hearts that know.

For every chill, a fire's spark,
In the silence, love leaves its mark.
Together we stand through the night,
In radiance bright, we hold the light.

The Tender Flicker of Winter's Heart

Amidst the frost, a flicker glows,
A tender light where warmth still flows.
In icy breaths, a secret shared,
The heart's soft pulse, a love declared.

Branches bare, yet dreams take flight,
In whispered tales of endless night.
The tender spark within us burns,
While winter's chill, to spring, returns.

Through fields of white, we roam and play,
As twilight fades, we find our way.
With every heartbeat, shadows dance,
In winter's arms, a sacred chance.

Together, we weave through snowy lanes,
Finding comfort in windowpanes.
With every flicker, joy imparts,
The tender warmth of winter's heart.

Dancing Shadows in Silent Nights

In silent nights, where shadows play,
Stories linger, lost in gray.
Each flicker, a memory spun,
Dancing under the watching sun.

With every step, the echoes sound,
In moonlit realms where dreams abound.
Drifting softly on winter's breeze,
A whisper floated through the trees.

In the stillness, our spirits soar,
Embracing the calm forever more.
Through winding paths, we weave and twine,
In shadows we find, our hearts align.

Under starlit skies, we chase the light,
Dancing together, holding tight.
In silent nights, our spirits thrived,
Amongst the shadows, love arrived.

Warmth's Resilience Against the Dark

When darkness falls and shadows loom,
Silent whispers chase the gloom.
Yet through the night, embers glow,
A warmth within that starts to grow.

With every heartbeat, hope persists,
A candle's flame in twilight's mist.
Resilience found in every spark,
A guiding light against the dark.

Through winter's chill, we find our way,
With love's embrace, brightening the day.
In icy grasp, we stand as one,
Warmth's resilience, never undone.

Together we face what lies ahead,
In every word, the warmth is spread.
In the quiet, we hear the call,
Of warmth's resilience, conquering all.

Tides of Light in Frigid Air

The moonlight dances on the snow,
Whispers of winter softly flow.
Stars like diamonds in the night,
Tides of light bring calm delight.

A breath of wind, a chill so clear,
Echoes of the past draw near.
The world wrapped tight in silver glow,
Promises of warmth beneath the snow.

Footprints trace a path so brave,
Nature's beauty, bold and grave.
Each flicker spark, a story told,
In this scene, the heart grows bold.

Frigid air and lights so bright,
Filling dreams with endless flight.
In winter's grasp, we find our way,
Tides of light, we long to stay.

Hearthside Reflections

Crackling embers, shadows dance,
In this moment, we take a chance.
Warmth surrounds, the fire glows,
Hearthside whispers, love bestows.

Stories shared, both old and new,
Memories linger, bright and true.
Time stands still as hearts align,
In golden glow, we intertwine.

Flickering light, a gentle guide,
Bringing all our hopes inside.
Laughter echoes, joy ignites,
Hearthside reflections, cozy nights.

As shadows grow, we draw near,
Comfort found, we shed our fear.
Together by the fire's embrace,
Hearthside love, our sacred space.

The Warmth of Yesterday's Fires

Fires once danced in golden hues,
Casting warmth in evening blues.
Memories linger, flames aglow,
Whispers of love from long ago.

In the glow of fading light,
Echoes call from depths of night.
Time may change, but hearts remain,
The warmth of yesterday's refrain.

Joyful laughter fills the air,
In every flicker, moments share.
Old stories told, a soothing balm,
In fires past, we find our calm.

Though seasons shift and embers die,
The warmth remains, we still comply.
In our hearts, the fire lives,
Yesterday's warmth, forever gives.

Shadows Cast by Candle's Flicker

In the night, the shadows play,
Candlelight leads the way.
Softly glowing, whispers near,
Secrets shared, moments dear.

Flickering flames, a dancing waltz,
In shadows cast, no time to halt.
Every flicker tells a tale,
Of love and loss, we set our sail.

Gentle warmth in a cozy room,
Light amidst the evening gloom.
Heartbeats echo, thoughts collide,
In the flicker, hope's our guide.

As shadows stretch, we draw so close,
In candle's light, we feel the most.
In every spark, our dreams take flight,
Shadows cast by candle's light.

Starlit Glances and Cozy Glows

Beneath the night, the stars collide,
Whispers dance where dreams abide.
Soft glimmers kiss the silent trees,
Wrapped in warmth, a gentle breeze.

Candles flicker, shadows play,
In cozy corners, lovers stay.
Hearts intertwined, a tender sigh,
In this stillness, moments fly.

Night's embrace, a silver hue,
A tapestry of me and you.
Each glance a spark, igniting fire,
In starlit realms, we both aspire.

Wrapped in love's eternal light,
We find our peace within the night.
Starlit glances, cozy glow,
Together here, our spirits grow.

Firespring of Solace

From embers born, the flames arise,
Infinite warmth beneath the skies.
Each flicker tells a tale divine,
In firespring's heart, we intertwine.

Laughter dances in the air,
Comfort found in every stare.
The crackling sound, a soothing balm,
In blazing light, our spirits calmed.

Embrace the heat, the passion flows,
A timeless love that ever grows.
In this sanctuary, we belong,
A melody, a whispered song.

Through storms and trials, we will stand,
With firespring's glow, hand in hand.
Solace found in every spark,
Guided forward through the dark.

Shadows of Specters Past

In twilight's glow, the shadows creep,
Memories linger, secrets keep.
Whispers echo through the trees,
Specters dance upon the breeze.

Faded laughs and silent cries,
Trace the lines where lost time lies.
In quiet corners, tales unfold,
Of dreams once bright, now threads of gold.

Glimmers of hope in the dim light,
Haunt the edges of the night.
With every step through time and space,
We find the strength to face the grace.

Shadows whisper, softly call,
Lessons learned through rise and fall.
In specters past, we find our way,
A brighter dawn, a brand new day.

Flames and Frost – A Dance of Duality

In fiery blaze, a passion burns,
While icy winds twist and churn.
A dance of heat and cooling breeze,
In nature's embrace, we find our ease.

Flames entwined with frosty breath,
Life and death in endless depth.
Each flicker shows a story's scope,
In duality, we find our hope.

From blazing hearts to chilling chill,
We ride the waves, we bend to will.
An ember's glow, a snowflake's fall,
Within this space, we hear the call.

Together we will forge and mend,
Through flames and frost, our souls ascend.
A dance of opposites, so grand,
In life's embrace, we take a stand.

Radiant Reflections on Frosted Glass

In morning light, a shimmer glows,
The frosted pane, where beauty flows.
Whispers of dreams, like silver threads,
Caught in the chill, where silence spreads.

A dance of hues, where shadows play,
Each breath reveals a bright display.
Echoes of warmth in winter's chill,
Through icy art, our hearts stand still.

The Lanterns of Quietude

In twilight's hush, the lanterns glow,
Soft amber light in the evening's flow.
Guiding the weary to restful places,
Cradled in time, with gentle embraces.

Whispers of night in a soothing breeze,
Carried along by rustling leaves.
Each glow a heartbeat, soft and near,
Filling the dark with warmth and cheer.

Firelight Lullabies

By crackling fire, we find our peace,
Warmth wraps around, as worries cease.
Flickers of light, a soothing embrace,
In dancing flames, we see our place.

Voices soft blend with the night,
As shadows waltz, a fabled sight.
Echoes of laughter, memories shared,
In firelight's glow, all hearts laid bare.

Glimpses of Warmth Beneath the Snow

Beneath the drifts, the earth sighs deep,
Winter's white blanket holds secrets to keep.
Echoes of spring lie sleeping tight,
In whispers of warmth, buried from sight.

Each flake a promise, a story to tell,
Of blooms yet to blossom, in winter's spell.
With patience we wait for the thaw to show,
The hidden life, beneath the snow.

Coals Beneath the Snowdrift

Hidden warmth in icy ground,
Coals aglow beneath the frost.
Breath of winter stirs around,
Nature whispers, never lost.

Silent nights, a hush so deep,
Stars above like scattered dreams.
In the dark, the hearth does keep,
Memories wrapped in silver beams.

Life persists where cold appears,
A flicker held beneath the chill.
Hope endures through frozen years,
Against the stillness, spirits thrill.

From this place, our visions grow,
Roots entwined in drifting white.
Coals beneath the snowdrift glow,
Guiding souls through longest night.

An Oath to the Season's Heart

With each falling leaf, a vow,
To cherish warmth and fleeting light.
In the chill, we gather now,
Bound together through the night.

Fires flicker, shadows dance,
Every spark ignites delight.
In the silence, take a chance,
Feel the pulse, embrace the night.

Hands held close, we share our dreams,
Whispers weave through autumn air.
In these moments, love redeems,
Offering solace, gentle care.

An oath made beneath the skies,
As we bask in ember's glow.
Through fleeting seasons, time flies,
In our hearts, forever know.

Solitude and Firelight

In the stillness, shadows play,
Firelight flickers, stories flow.
Silence cradles night and day,
As memories begin to grow.

Each crackle speaks of days gone by,
Dancing flames, a warm embrace.
Underneath this spectral sky,
Solitude finds its sacred space.

In the glow, I find my peace,
Thoughts like embers softly rise.
Time stands still, all cares release,
In this hearth, I touch the skies.

Here among the wood and light,
Life unfolds like stories told.
Embers fade into the night,
In solitude, my heart is bold.

Ember Gaze on Still Waters

By the shore where silence reigns,
Reflections shimmer, soft and bright.
Embers dance like fireless flames,
Painting whispers in the night.

Gaze into the depths so clear,
Where stars descend to gently play.
Each ripple holds a memory dear,
As night embraces the fading day.

Beneath the moon's tender glow,
Hearts entwined with nature's grace.
In the stillness, time moves slow,
Carrying dreams from place to place.

Ember gazes blend with skies,
On still waters, spirits soar.
In the quiet, love belies,
As we linger forevermore.

Flickering Shadows of December

In the chill of winter's breath,
Shadows dance on frozen trails.
Whispers of old tales linger,
Wrapped in frost, the night prevails.

Moonlight glimmers on the trees,
Casting secrets on the ground.
Footprints left from long ago,
Echoes in the silence found.

Candles flicker in the dark,
Casting warmth through cold despair.
Memories float like drifting snow,
Softly weaving in the air.

In December's tender hold,
Time stands still, a gentle pause.
Each shadow tells a story true,
Cozy nights, a love because.

Dance of the Distant Stars

High above the world we know,
Stars are twinkling far away.
A dance of light in velvet skies,
Highlighting dreams that gently sway.

Every twinkle tells a tale,
Of wishes whispered deep within.
Guiding hearts through darkened nights,
Showing us where hope begins.

Galaxies collide and swirl,
Painting stories bright and bold.
In this cosmic waltz we find,
The mysteries that time has told.

Let us gaze upon the night,
Holding hands beneath the glow.
In this dance of distant stars,
Together we will always flow.

Twinkling Lights on Snowy Nights

Snowflakes fall like soft confetti,
Blanketing the world in white.
Twinkling lights adorn the streets,
Bringing magic to the night.

Children laugh and angels play,
Building dreams with gloved hands.
Each breath clouds in arctic air,
As joy unravels winter's strands.

Candles flicker in each home,
Windowpanes aglow with cheer.
Warming hearts on snowy nights,
Wrapping all in love sincere.

Underneath the starlit skies,
Hope and laughter intertwine.
Twinkling lights in all their grace,
Guide us through the soft divine.

Memories Wrapped in Wool

A blanket thick, a cozy thread,
Whispers of the past reside.
Each stitch holds a memory,
In woolen warmth, our hearts abide.

Gathered close around the fire,
Stories shared with every gaze.
Laughter echoes through the room,
In this soft and gentle haze.

Wrapped in comfort, time stands still,
Childhood dreams in every fold.
Weaves of love and bittersweet,
In every thread, the stories told.

As seasons change, we hold it tight,
This fabric stitched of days gone by.
Memories wrapped in wool embrace,
A treasured bond that will not die.

The Luminous Whisper of Frosty Evenings

The moonlight dances on the snow,
Whispers of winter softly flow.
Stars are jewels in the night sky,
As chilly breezes drift on by.

Silent trees wear coats of white,
While shadows linger, holding tight.
A whisper speaks of peace untold,
As frosty tales begin to unfold.

Under a blanket, dreams ignite,
The world transforms in silver light.
In the hush of night, hearts revive,
In frosty evenings, we feel alive.

Each breath creates a cloud of mist,
A fragile moment not to miss.
In the luminous glow, spirits soar,
In winter's embrace, we find much more.

Firelight Tales in Frozen Air

Gathered round the crackling flame,
Stories told with love's sweet name.
Outside the world is cold and still,
Inside our hearts, a warming thrill.

Embers dance in the twilight glow,
Casting shadows, soft and slow.
Laughter echoes, fills the room,
As flickering lights chase away gloom.

Frozen nights may chill the bone,
But here we find we are not alone.
With every tale, the spirits rise,
In firelight's warmth, we find our skies.

As memories wrap like a cozy quilt,
In this space, our fears are spilt.
Firelight tales, forever we share,
In frozen air, we find our flare.

Shimmers in the Winter Wood

In the woods where silence reigns,
Snowflakes fall like whispered chains.
Softly drifting, the branches sigh,
Beneath the weight of a twilight sky.

Each shimmer sparkles, pure and bright,
A tapestry woven with pure delight.
Footsteps crunch on the frosted ground,
As nature's breath creates a sound.

Icicles hang like crystal dreams,
Reflecting moonlight in silver beams.
Here in this grove, all worries cease,
In the winter woods, we find our peace.

Nature's canvas, a sight to behold,
Stories of winter patiently told.
Among the trees, our spirits twine,
In shimmers of magic, we intertwine.

Kindling Solace Amidst the Snow

Amidst the snow, a quiet place,
Where stillness offers sweet embrace.
Kindling solace, hearts align,
In winter's arms, our souls entwine.

The world outside, a painted white,
With every breath, a spark of light.
In the gentle hush, we come alive,
In this sanctuary, we truly thrive.

Frosty windows, a world anew,
Each flake a memory born anew.
With every glance, a smile ignites,
As warmth surrounds the coldest nights.

Kindling hope in the frozen air,
Love's quiet glow, a tender care.
Amidst the snow, we find our way,
In winter's kindness, we choose to stay.

A Radiant Beacon in Hibernal Silence

In the stillness of the night,
A gleam breaks the cold gray,
Luminous warmth on the frost,
Hearts awaken from their sway.

Through the silence softly sings,
A light that dances and sways,
Guiding lost souls like fireflies,
In the deep of winter's maze.

Beneath the blanket of white,
Hope flickers in the dark,
Wrapped in dreams and whispers,
Its glow leaves a lasting mark.

In hibernal silence spread,
The beacon shines bright,
A promise of spring's return,
After the long, mystical night.

Flames that Defy the Icy Breath

In the heart of winter's grip,
Flames leap high, undeterred,
Whispers of warmth in the air,
Against the chill, they've stirred.

Challenging the icy breath,
They dance with fiery grace,
Bright embers, fierce and bold,
In this frozen embrace.

Each flicker holds its own tale,
Of warmth that cannot fade,
A defiance in the snow,
An art in flames displayed.

As shadows merge with light,
Courage ignites the cold,
For even in the darkest night,
A fire's heart beats bold.

A Melting Promise Beneath the Stars

Underneath a sky so vast,
Stars shimmer with silent grace,
A promise made to the night,
In this tranquil, sacred space.

Snowflakes tumble, soft and light,
As warmth begins to rise,
Each droplet whispers dreams,
Beneath the vast, starry skies.

A melting promise in the air,
Hope dances on the breeze,
Nature's silent symphony,
A gentle song that frees.

As daybreak calls, a new embrace,
With golden rays that chase,
The wintry hold begins to fade,
And life returns with grace.

The Hearth's Lullaby in Frosty Grasp

In the corner, embers glow,
A lullaby's tender sound,
Wrapped in warmth, shadows play,
In the hearth, comfort found.

Frosty tendrils weave around,
Yet inside, the glow is bright,
As stories mingle with the flames,
In the soothing winter night.

The hearth sings a soft refrain,
Of love and peace, so deep,
A sanctuary from the storm,
Where worries fade to sleep.

In this cocoon of warmth and light,
Hold dear those moments passed,
For within the frosty grasp,
The hearth's lullaby will last.

Beneath the Boughs of Silent Pines

Whispers drift on gentle breeze,
Among the trunks, the world finds peace.
Soft shadows dance in muted light,
Nature's hush, a sweet delight.

Mossy carpets, emerald green,
Nestled roots like dreams unseen.
The air is filled with pine's embrace,
In this stillness, time finds grace.

Birds sing softly, notes take flight,
A symphony of pure delight.
Beneath the boughs, where hearts align,
In quiet moments, love does shine.

With every breath, the forest breathes,
A tapestry of life it weaves.
In sacred space where spirits roam,
Beneath the pines, we find our home.

A Lantern's Call in the Dark

Flickering flames in the midnight air,
Guiding wanderers with tender care.
A beacon bright against the night,
Hope is carried in its light.

Shadows lengthen, whispers creep,
Secrets hide where dreamers sleep.
The lantern's glow, a steadfast friend,
In the hush, our fears will mend.

Each flicker tells a story near,
Of journeys' end and paths unclear.
With every spark, the heart takes flight,
In the darkness, there shines light.

So follow where the lantern leads,
Through tangled thoughts and quiet needs.
In the embrace of its warm glow,
We find the courage all must know.

When Snow Meets the Flame

Snowflakes fall, a gentle sigh,
Whispers soft as they drift by.
In winter's hush, a dance begins,
Where cold meets warmth, as silence wins.

Embers glisten, crackles loud,
In the hearth, a glowing shroud.
The white drifts swirl, a winter's dream,
While fire's heart starts to beam.

Together they create a spark,
In the stillness, love leaves its mark.
With every flake that falls in grace,
The flame ignites, a warm embrace.

For in the clash of frost and fire,
Lives a beauty, hearts desire.
When snow meets flame in bright array,
Magic dances through the day.

Ashes of Yesterday's Warmth

In quiet corners, shadows fade,
Where memories linger, softly laid.
With whispered tales of days gone by,
We hold the past with a gentle sigh.

Ashes fall, touching the ground,
In their silence, a comfort found.
Fragments of laughter, echoes sweet,
Remind us all of love's heartbeat.

Through time's embrace, we learn to part,
Yet carry warmth within the heart.
Though flames may dim, their glow remains,
In every loss, a love sustains.

So let us cherish every trace,
Of warmth that time cannot erase.
For ashes, too, hold stories bright,
Of yesterday's warmth, a guiding light.

A Symphony of Flames and Frost

In shadows dance the flames so bright,
A flicker warms the crisp, cold night.
Winter's breath, a silent sigh,
As embers fade, the stars reply.

Whispers of frost on windows cling,
Nature's hush, the heart's soft spring.
A balance found in fire and ice,
With every crackle, a paradise.

Glowing orange, the hearth's embrace,
Crystal silence, a fragile grace.
Together they twirl, a bold romance,
In the blaze, we find our chance.

Yet from the chill, new life will rise,
As seasons shift beneath the skies.
So let the symphony play on strong,
For fire and frost deserve their song.

Winter Whispers in the Glow

In the stillness, soft voices weave,
Winter's whispers, a tale to believe.
Beneath the moon's tender, pale light,
The world holds its breath in the quiet night.

Huddled in blankets, by fireside glow,
Each flicker tells stories of old we know.
The crackling wood sings of yesterdays,
As frost-kissed branches begin to sway.

Snowflakes dance like dreams in flight,
Transforming the earth with a blanket of white.
They settle down, in silence they rest,
Each one unique, a marvel, a guest.

Voices of winter, soft and low,
In the heart, they plant seeds to grow.
As the chill settles into our bones,
We find warmth in whispers, in hushed undertones.

Halo of Warmth in a Cold World

Surrounded by cold, a flicker ignites,
A halo of warmth on the frostbitten nights.
In the heart of the chill, we gather near,
The laughter we share, the love that's clear.

Through windows adorned with crystals bright,
We watch the world wrapped in shimmering light.
Outside the storm rages, fierce and wild,
Inside, we cherish the warmth, like a child.

With each passing moment, the firelight glows,
Collecting our dreams like soft-falling snows.
Together we rise, as shadows take flight,
In a cold world, we are the light.

Bound by the warmth of our spirits combined,
Through chill and through darkness, we remain aligned.
As the whispers of winter swirl all around,
In the halo of warmth, our solace is found.

Illuminated Footprints in the Snow

Beneath the stars, where silence sings,
Illuminated footprints show where it brings.
Through the blanket of snow, a journey unfolds,
Each step a story, a tale retold.

The soft crunch echoes the path we've traced,
In the winter's embrace, we find our place.
The moon paints the scene with silver and glow,
As shadows linger in the white, soft snow.

Frosty breath hangs like dreams in the air,
Illuminated moments, gentle and rare.
Each tiny flake adds to this scene,
A canvas of wonder, serene and pristine.

In the stillness, we pause, reflect on the way,
With footprints behind us, our hearts start to sway.
For every step taken, in magical light,
Leaves traces of warmth, through the cold of the night.

The Cradle of Embered Dreams

In the shadows where whispers sigh,
A cradle rocks beneath the sky.
Dreams are woven with gentle thread,
In glowing coals, our wishes spread.

Softly sighs the night's embrace,
Stars twinkle with a mystic grace.
Beneath the moon's pale silver gleam,
We drift away on hope's sweet dream.

With each breath, the embers rise,
Lighting up our secret skies.
Wrapped in warmth, we find our peace,
In this cradle, our fears release.

As morning breaks with tender light,
Our dreams take flight into the bright.
With every ember, every gleam,
We nurture life, our endless dream.

Frosty Boughs and Flickering Flames

Beneath the boughs where frost does cling,
A flicker dances, warmth to bring.
The hush of winter cradles night,
As embers glow with soft delight.

Whispers flow on icy air,
Stories told with loving care.
In the flicker, shadows play,
As frosty branches sway and sway.

Beneath the stars that brightly shine,
Flames entwine with the pine.
With every crackle, hearts unite,
Against the chill, we find the light.

Echoes warm the coldest hour,
With frosty boughs, we find our power.
In flickering flames, we feel alive,
Together still, we will survive.

Snowflakes and Hearth Stones

Snowflakes tumble, soft and white,
Snowy whispers kiss the night.
Hearth stones glow with amber warmth,
Crackling tales in winter's charm.

In the quiet, memories stir,
As every flake begins to blur.
Layered deep on earth's embrace,
Nature's quilt, our sacred space.

Laughter dances with the light,
As families gather, hearts so bright.
Beside the fire, we tell our tales,
As snowflakes drift on winter gales.

Together here, we watch and dream,
In this stillness, life's sweet theme.
With every hearth stone's gentle glow,
Love's warmth and peace begin to flow.

Through Windows Frosted and Bright

Through windows frosted, visions glow,
Lights cascade on shimmering snow.
With every frame, a story told,
Of warmth and love, of courage bold.

The world outside is crisp and cold,
But warmth within breaks winter's hold.
Together we watch the snowflakes dance,
In quiet moments of sweet romance.

Children giggle as they roam,
While visions of joy light up our home.
Through windows bright, the heart takes flight,
In every shadow, we find our light.

So here we stay, in love's embrace,
Through frosted glass, we find our place.
With each heartbeat, memories ignite,
Together forever, through day and night.

Warm Shadows in the Winter Wilderness

Beneath the snowy pines, we tread,
Footprints soft in winter's spread.
In the hush, our whispers play,
Casting warmth against the gray.

Frosted branches, whispers near,
Every breath, a cloud appears.
In the twilight's fading light,
Shadows dance, a hopeful sight.

The chill wraps tight, but hearts are bold,
A tapestry of tales retold.
In the silence, love will thrive,
Through warm shadows, we're alive.

Stars emerge as day departs,
Painting skies with starlit arts.
Together, we embrace the night,
In this wilderness, pure delight.

The Soft Glow Against the Dimming Day

As the sun dips low, it calls,
Casting gold on ancient walls.
The soft glow like a gentle sigh,
Whispers secrets, as day goes by.

Candles flicker in the dusk,
Fleeting moments, sweet and husk.
Each shadow dances in the room,
A silent symphony of bloom.

Waves of color, a canvas bright,
Emerging dreams in fading light.
The stars awaken one by one,
Kissing earth as day is done.

In twilight's arms, we find our place,
A tender touch, a warm embrace.
Together, we greet the coming night,
Captured in this gentle sight.

Hearts Ignited in a Frozen World

In the frost, our spirits blaze,
Igniting embers through the haze.
Each heartbeat makes the cold retreat,
Wrapped in warmth, we're incomplete.

Frozen landscapes, pure and bright,
Yet inside blooms a fiery light.
Together we will break the chill,
With passion's spark, our dreams fulfill.

Icy winds may chill the air,
But love's warmth, a gentle flare.
In every glance, a spark ignites,
Turning darkness into lights.

Through winter's grasp, we boldly roam,
In this frozen world, we find a home.
Hearts aflame, we dance and soar,
For love endures forevermore.

Fireside Whispers

By the fire, the stories flow,
Dancing flames, an amber glow.
Each whisper carries, soft and clear,
Sharing dreams, and drawing near.

The crackling wood, a soothing song,
In this warmth, we all belong.
Under the stars, we laugh and sigh,
As shadows play, time drifts by.

In the night, our voices weave,
Tales of love, hope, and believe.
Embers flicker, memories made,
In this circle, fears will fade.

Fireside whispers fill the air,
Binding hearts with tender care.
As the night embraces deep,
In this warmth, our souls shall keep.

Light in the Whispering Woods

In the hush of morning light,
Shadows dance beneath the trees.
Whispers brush the leaves so bright,
Nature sings on gentle breeze.

Softly glows the forest floor,
With the laughter of the stream.
Every path opens a door,
To the magic and the dream.

Sunbeams sprinkle through the green,
Kissing petals, pure delight.
Every nook a sacred scene,
Echoes of the day and night.

Here in silence, heart finds peace,
Wrapped in nature's sweet embrace.
In this place, all worries cease,
Lost in woods of calm and grace.

Dances of Frost and Flame

Underneath the pale moon's glow,
Frosty whispers weave through trees.
Flames of autumn start to show,
Dancing gently in the breeze.

Crimson leaves, the earth's delight,
Crisp and crackling with each step.
In the chill of velvet night,
Nature weaves her secret prep.

Whirling sparks against the night,
Frosty diamonds in the air.
Fires flicker with pure delight,
Joyful warmth beyond compare.

Frost and flame in sacred dance,
Joining hearts with each embrace.
In the stillness, take a chance,
Find your place in nature's grace.

Hearthfire Memories

In the glow of flickering light,
Stories woven, hearts unfold.
Laughter dances through the night,
Each memory a thread of gold.

Flickering flames that softly play,
Whispers of the past return.
Tales of joy, of love's warm sway,
In the hearth, we feel the burn.

Time is captured in this space,
Echoes lingering in the air.
In this moment, gentle grace,
Comfort lingers everywhere.

A tapestry of times gone by,
Shared with those we hold so dear.
In the hearth, warm love will lie,
Wrapping all in laughter's cheer.

Kindling Hope in the Dark Cold

In the shadows, whispers rise,
Flickers of a warm embrace.
Hope ignites within our eyes,
Filling every lonely space.

Through the chill, our spirits soar,
Grains of light from dreams we weave.
In the dark, we find the core,
Of the strength we dare believe.

Gathered close, our hearts entwined,
Stories shared will light our way.
In each moment, hope defined,
Kindles warmth in coldest grey.

As the night gives way to dawn,
Brighter days will soon unfold.
In our hearts, the fire is drawn,
Kindling hope through dark and cold.

Milton Keynes UK
Ingram Content Group UK Ltd.
UKHW022144111124
451073UK00007B/191

9 789916 944141